ELVIS WAS A
PUZZLING MAN . . .

His life was full of contradictions, and though fan magazines wrote endless articles about him and fans felt as though they knew him intimately, there seemed always to be so much more to know.

Here's your chance to test your Presley knowledge. Through jumbles and anagrams, true-or-false teasers, multiple choice and matching, you can have fun discovering vital statistics, facts about his records, movies, concerts, in-person appearances, his army life, love life and even his death. It's all here in

THE
ELVIS PRESLEY
QUIZBOOK

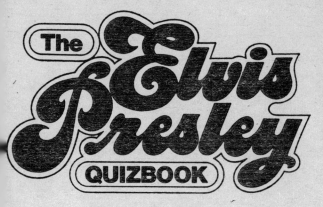

The Elvis Presley QUIZBOOK

Bruce M. Nash

WARNER BOOKS

A Warner Communications Company

Warner Books are
distributed in the
United Kingdom by

NEW ENGLISH LIBRARY

WARNER BOOKS EDITION

Copyright © 1978 by Bruce M. Nash
All rights reserved

ISBN 0-446-89823-6

Cover photo of Zolimodel Sara Truslow by
Co Rentmeester © People Weekly

Photograph section designed by Marsha Gold

Warner Books, Inc., 75 Rockefeller Plaza, New York, N.Y.
10019

A Warner Communications Company

Printed in the United States of America

Not associated with Warner Press, Inc., of Anderson, Indiana

First Printing: July, 1978

10 9 8 7 6 5 4 3 2

To my precious daughter,
Robyn, who will always be
Elvis's Number One fan

ACKNOWLEDGMENTS

Special thanks to Karen Newmark, Deborah Wirthington, Tony Wharton, Cindy Bullwinkel, and Lynn Tuckwood for their timely research assistance. Above all else, I am eternally grateful for both the encouragement offered and the confidence shown by my wife, Sophie, daughters Robyn and Jenny, mother and father, grandparents, brother Greg, sister Mary, brother Gus, nephew Sean, Aunt Kate, and dear friends Rita and Jim Graham.

CONTENTS

THE
ELVIS PRESLEY
QUIZBOOK

REMEMBERING ELVIS

The Elvis Presley Quizbook is a sentimental tribute to America's greatest musical entertainer. It offers the millions who loved him the opportunity to nostalgically reminisce about "the King" and his music, movies, television appearances, concerts, and personal life.

Elvis was far more than a mere show business phenomenon. He was the flesh-and-blood personification of "The American Dream" . . . the dirt-poor country boy who wiggled and warbled his way to unprecedented fame and fortune.

Yet Elvis never forgot his humble beginnings. He bestowed a sprawling Memphis estate and lavish gifts upon his beloved parents, performed numerous benefit concerts, treated friends and strangers alike to surprise presents, and continued entertaining millions of adoring fans all over the world on a breakneck schedule long after money had ceased to be an objct for him.

Elvis was a genuinely likable person. You could tell from his boyish grin that he was every bit as friendly and sincere as he appeared to be. Boyfriends and husbands didn't even seem to mind if their mates screamed with frenzied excitement over Elvis. After all, they liked him, too.

Elvis was "the King" in an entertainment world filled with giants. His untimely passing has left a gaping void in our lives. But, even in death, Elvis will continue to live on . . . in his music, in his movies, and in our memories.

1. VITAL STATISTICS

1. Where was Elvis born?

2. What was his birthdate?

3. What was his seldom-heard middle name?

4. What color were his eyes?

5. What was the natural color of his hair?

6. How tall was he?

7. Approximately how much did Elvis weigh when he was in peak physical condition?

8. What church did he attend?

9. What was the highest grade he completed in school?

10. In what contact sport did he excel?

1. ANSWERS

1. Tupelo, Mississippi

2. January 8, 1935

3. Aron

4. Blue

5. Dark-blond

6. Six feet tall

7. 175 pounds

8. The Assembly of God, a Pentecostal sect

9. Twelfth

10. Karate

2. GROWING UP

1. Where did Elvis gain his first singing experience?

2. Ten-yearold Elvis won second prize at the 1945 Mississippi-Alabama Fair and Dairy Show singing about a dog. What was the canine's name?

3. How much money did Elvis receive for his runner-up finish?

4. How old was Elvis when he received his first guitar as a birthday present from his parents?

5. How much did the guitar cost?

6. How old was Elvis when his family moved to Memphis?

7. What high school did he attend?

8. What were his two favorite subjects in school?

9. What color outfits did Elvis like to wear as a teenager in Memphis?

10. What organized sport did Elvis play in high school?

2. ANSWERS

1. In church

2. "Old Shep"

3. $5.00

4. Twelve

5. $12.95

6. Thirteen

7. Humes High School

8. Shop and R.O.T.C.

9. Pink and black

10. Football

3. EARLY WIGGLES

1. How old was Elvis when he made his first amateur recording?

2. How much did it cost him?

3. What two songs did he record?

4. Where did he make this historic recording?

5. Why did Elvis make the recording?

6. What type of work was Elvis engaged in at the time?

7. What company did he work for?

8. Who was Elvis's early singing idol?

9. Who backed up Elvis on guitar and

bass fiddle on his first professional recording?

10. Who was the drummer Elvis later added to his back-up group?

11. What was the name of the group?

12. Elvis created a new "rockabilly" sound. What two musical styles were combined to create this unique blend of music?

13. What well-known country music show told Elvis he should quit singing and go back to driving a truck?

14. On what Shreveport-based musical program did Elvis appear as a regular?

15. What were Elvis's nicknames during the early days of his professional career?

16. How many singles did Elvis cut for his first professional recording company?

17. What entrepreneur took over as Elvis's personal manager in late 1955 and re-

mained with him until "the King" 's
dying day?

18. How much did RCA pay to buy up
Elvis's contract in 1955?

19. What did Elvis purchase with the extra
bonus money he received as part of
the deal?

20. What TV talent show rejected Elvis as
a possible contestant after watching
him audition?

3. ANSWERS

1. Eighteen

2. $4.00

3. "My Happiness" and "That's When Your Heartaches Begin"

4. At the Memphis Recording Service

5. It was a birthday present for his mother

6. He was a delivery-truck driver

7. Crown Electric Company

8. Dean Martin

9. Scotty Moore (guitar) and Bill Black (bass fiddle)

10. D. J. Fontana

11. The Blue Moon Boys

12. White hillbilly and Negro blues

13. "Grand Ole Opry"

14. "Louisiana Hayride"

15. "The Hillbilly Cat" and "King Of Western Bop"

16. Five

17. Colonel Tom Parker

18. $35,000, plus a $5,000 bonus

19. A Cadillac

20. "Arthur Godfrey's Talent Scouts"

4. GOLDEN OLDIES

1. What was Elvis's first gold record?

2. How many Elvis singles sold more than a million copies?

3. What Elvis platter sold more than eight million copies?

4. How many gold albums are credited to Elvis?

5. What mid-1960 release grossed over $1.25 million dollars in sales within the first three weeks of its initial distribution?

6. After failing to produce a gold record for seven years, Elvis ended his long drought with a million-seller in 1969. What was the title of this gold single?

7. What other gold record did Elvis follow up with during this same year?

8. What top-selling Elvis album sold five million copies?

9. Which one of the following singles was **not** a Presley gold record?: (a) "Return To Sender" (b) "Can't Help Falling In Love" (c) "That's All Right (Mama)" (d) "Don't"

10. What was Elvis's last gold record?

4. ANSWERS

1. "Heartbreak Hotel"

2. Fifty-five

3. "Hound Dog"/"Don't Be Cruel"

4. Twenty-four

5. "It's Now Or Never"

6. "Suspicious Minds"

7. "Don't Cry, Daddy"

8. "Blue Hawaii"

9. (c)

10. "My Boy"

5. MOVIE MAGIC

1. How many movies did Elvis appear in?

2. What producer gave Elvis his first screen test?

3. What actor of "Dobie Gillis" TV fame appeared with Elvis in his screen test?

4. What was Elvis's first motion picture?

5. Who co-starred with Elvis in his screen debut?

6. What color was Elvis's hair in his first movie?

7. What studio produced Elvis's first film?

8. Which two Elvis movies were documentaries?

9. Which three of Elvis's movies were filmed in black-and-white?

10. What was the first Elvis film to be released in color?

11. What was Elvis's final movie?

12. What was the original title of **Love Me Tender?**

13. Why was the title of the film changed?

14. In what film did Elvis play a dual role?

15. In which one of Elvis's movies did his parents appear as extras?

16. How many films did Elvis shoot in Hawaii?

17. Which one of Elvis's film roles was originally intended for Marlon Brando?

18. During his moviemaking peak, what was Elvis's usual salary and piece of the action for each film he made?

19. What was the only movie in which Elvis was killed?

20. What two Elvis films included the names of cities in their titles?

21. What was the only film in which Elvis wore a beard?

22. What was the last movie in which Elvis played a fictional character?

23. What was Elvis's most financially-successful film?

24. What was the first movie in which Elvis did not sing?

25. Approximately how much money did Elvis's films gross in worldwide distribution?

5. ANSWERS

1. Thirty-three

2. Hal Wallis

3. Frank Faylen, who played Dobie's be-leaguered dad

4. **Love Me Tender**

5. Richard Egan and Debra Paget

6. Blond

7. Twentieth Century-Fox

8. **That's The Way It Is** and **Elvis On Tour**

9. **Love Me Tender, Jailhouse Rock,** and **King Creole**

10. **Loving You**

11. **Elvis On Tour**

12. **The Reno Brothers**

13. The studio wanted to capitalize on the enormous popularity of Elvis's hit record, "Love Me Tender"

14. **Kissin' Cousins**

15. **Loving You**

16. Two, **Blue Hawaii** and **Paradise—Hawaiian Style**

17. Pacer Burton, in **Flaming Star**

18. One million dollars and 50 percent of the gross

19. **Love Me Tender**

20. **Fun In Acapulco** and **Viva Las Vegas**

21. **Charro!**

22. **The Trouble With Girls**

23. **Blue Hawaii**

24. Charro!

25. $150 million dollars

6. WITH ALL MY HEART

1. In "It's Now Or Never," what happened to Elvis's heart when he first saw his girl's tender smile?

2. What is Elvis's heart made out of in "Any Way You Want Me"?

3. In "I Was The One," after Elvis taught his girl how to kiss, touch his cheek, and cry when she wanted him under her spell, what did she wind up doing to him?

4. What are Elvis and his girl going to sweep out of their hearts to "Patch It Up"?

5. What is "Poor Boy" 's heart filled with?

6. Whose tears will tear at Elvis's heart

forever when he and his wife go their "Separate Ways"?

7. Besides steel nerves, what do you need to win a fortune in "Viva Las Vegas"?

8. In "Wooden Heart," what would Elvis do if his girl said good-bye?

9. In "Follow That Dream," what is it time to do when your heart becomes weary?

10. Where will Elvis wish in each fountain and pray that his girl will return?

6. ANSWERS

1. It was captured

2. Clay

3. Breaking his heart

4. Cobwebs

5. Dreams and memories

6. His daughter's

7. A strong heart

8. Cry, maybe die

9. Sing a song

10. In the "Heart of Rome"

7. FAMILY ALBUM

1. What was the name of Elvis's twin brother who died shortly after birth?

2. What is the name of Elvis's father?

3. What is so unusual about his "daddy" 's middle name?

4. What was the name of Elvis's mother?

5. What was the tragic similarity between Elvis's and his mother's untimely deaths?

6. What inscription did Elvis have carved on his mother's tombstone?

7. What was the name of Elvis's step-mother?

8. What two relatives lived with Elvis

while he was stationed overseas in the army?

9. In what year was Elvis married?

10. Whom did he marry?

11. How long did his bride-to-be live with Elvis and his father and stepmother in their Memphis mansion before the wedding took place?

12. What is the name of Elvis's daughter?

13. In what year was Elvis divorced?

14. How many times did Elvis re-marry?

15. To whom was Elvis engaged at the time of his death?

7. ANSWERS

1. Jesse Garon

2. Vernon

3. His middle name is Elvis

4. Gladys

5. They both died at the age of forty-two

6. "She Was The Sunshine Of Our House"

7. Davada "Dee" Stanley

8. His father Vernon and grandmother Minnie Mae

9. 1967 (May 1)

10. Priscilla Beaulieu

11. From 1960 to 1967

12. Lisa Marie

13. 1973 (October 9)

14. He never re-married

15. Ginger Alden

8. REQUEST LINE

1. Since the beginning of the world, who, along with a "Hard Headed Woman," has been causing trouble?

2. What kind of tears was Elvis "Crying In The Chapel"?

3. What did Elvis keep to remember "Anything That's Part Of You"?

4. How will Mister Crawfish taste if he's fried or boiled just right?

5. What does Elvis say you can treat him like if you'll only "Love Me"?

6. What is the only thing Elvis's "Rock-A-Hula Baby" wants to do?

7. What will Elvis follow as he's "Ridin' The Rainbow" to his girl?

8. What does Elvis want his girl to put around his neck so he can be her "Teddy Bear"?

9. What does Elvis say to do if you don't want him to be as cold as ice?

10. What was buzzin' in Elvis's ear and brain before it stung him all over?

8. ANSWERS

1. A soft-hearted man

2. Tears of joy

3. A hair ribbon

4. Sweeter than sugar

5. A fool

6. Dance

7. His star

8. A chain

9. "Treat Me Nice"

10. A honeybee

9. PRIVATE GLIMPSES

Which of the following statements about Elvis's personal life are true?

1. Elvis rarely stayed up past midnight.

2. Constantly surrounded by friends, Elvis was never lonely.

3. Elvis always paid his full income tax, never looking for tax shelters or loop-holes.

4. In retrospect, Elvis did not think very highly of the movies he made.

5. Elvis wore sideburns as a teenager to cover up the acne on his face.

6. Elvis was deathly afraid of guns.

7. Elvis dyed his hair black after it had turned prematurely gray.

8. Elvis didn't drink alcoholic beverages, but he was a heavy smoker.

9. Elvis and his mother did not get along too well when she was alive.

10. Elvis gained a lot of weight in his later years because he had a special weakness for gourmet foods.

9. ANSWERS

1. False. Elvis stayed up until all hours of the night

2. False. Elvis was a very lonely person

3. True

4. True

5. False. He wore them to look older and to attract attention

6. False. He was a gun fancier

7. True

8. False. Elvis didn't smoke

9. False. Elvis worshiped his mother

10. False. Elvis's weakness was for "junk food."

10. MUSICAL MEMORIES

1. What five "Good Luck Charm(s)" is Elvis willing to forsake for you?

2. What sad news does Elvis tell "My Boy"?

3. What is the only thing that's left between Elvis and his wife after they go their "Separate Ways"?

4. In "All Shook Up," what is Elvis itching like?

5. What type of music were Elvis's mother and papa listening to while he was being "Raised On Rock"?

6. Why is Elvis feeling so "Hurt"?

7. In "That's All Right (Mama)," what do

Elvis's momma and papa warn him about the girl he's foolin' with?

8. Where does Elvis's girl live in "I Got A Woman"?

9. In "Little Sister," with whom does big sister sneak out of the show when Elvis goes to buy some candy?

10. What was the reason for living Elvis's wife took away from him in "You Gave Me A Mountain"?

10. ANSWERS

1. A four-leaf clover, an old horseshoe, a silver dollar, a rabbit's foot, and a lucky penny

2. That he (Elvis) and his wife don't love each other anymore

3. Memories they shared

4. A man in a fuzzy tree

5. His mother was listening to Beethoven's Fifth and Mozart's sonatas; his father was listening to country songs

6. Because his girl lied to him

7. That she isn't any good for him

8. Way across town

9. Jim Dandy

10. His little baby boy

11. SCREEN TESTS

1. Why was Elvis placed on probation in **Wild In The Country?**

2. What type of work did Elvis choose over his upper-class family's pineapple business in **Blue Hawaii?**

3. What did Elvis have to do to win the wager his army buddies had made in **G.I. Blues?**

4. Who did Elvis mistake the king's daughter for in **Harum Scarum?**

5. What did the Air Force want to build atop Pappy Tatum's Big Smokey Mountain in **Kissin' Cousins?**

6. What did Elvis and his girl volunteer for in the conclusion of **It Happened At The World's Fair?**

7. What did Elvis want to buy with the money he was earning as a nightclub singer in **Girls! Girls! Girls!?**

8. Of the Los Angeles 500, the Santa Fe Road Race, or the Dallas Cross-Country, which was the race Elvis won in **Spinout?**

9. What did Elvis's nightclub boss secretly arrange for him to do in **Girl Happy?**

10. Where did Elvis discover the missing gold in **Tickle Me?**

11. What did Elvis and his Navajo Indian friends mistakenly slaughter and eat at a party in **Stay Away, Joe?**

12. Why did Elvis change both his appearance and his personality in **Live A Little, Love A Little?**

13. During what decade did **The Trouble With Girls** take place?

14. What was Elvis's occupation before he became a singing star in **Loving You?**

15. What did Uncle Gerard have Elvis arrested for in **Double Trouble?**

11. ANSWERS

1. He seriously injured his brother in a fight

2. He worked for a tourist agency

3. He had to spend the night in the apartment of a local cabaret dancer

4. A slave girl

5. A missile base

6. The space program

7. A sailboat, the **West Wind**

8. The Santa Fe Road Race

9. Keep watch over his daughter while she was on Easter vacation in Fort Lauderdale

10. In a cellar wall

11. The bull they were using to stud a herd of heifers

12. He was working as a commercial photographer for two different bosses, one a conservative, the other a liberal

13. The 1920s

14. He was a truck driver

15. Kidnapping his niece

12. FAMOUS FIRSTS

1. Who was the first person to record Elvis's singing?

2. What was the first song Elvis ever recorded?

3. What was the name of his first professional recording company?

4. What was the first record he cut for them?

5. Who was the first disc jockey to play the "A" side of this platter?

6. Who was the first disc jockey to play the "B" or flip side of this single?

7. What was Elvis's first single on the RCA label?

8. What was his first RCA single **not** to have been previously recorded on his old label?

9. What was the color of Elvis's first Cadillac?

10. Who was Elvis's first personal manager?

11. In what year did Elvis make his first motion picture?

12. What movie was billed as Elvis's "first big dramatic singing role"?

13. What was the first movie in which Elvis appeared with black hair?

14. What was Elvis's first number-one hit single?

15. Which one of the following songs was **not** on Elvis's first album?: (a) "Money Honey" (b) "Love Me" (c) "Blue Suede Shoes" (d) "I Love You Because."

16. What was the title of Elvis's first motion picture soundtrack LP album?

17. In what song did Elvis record his first piano accompaniment?

18. With whom did Elvis sing his first movie duet?

19. How old was Elvis when he made his first million?

20. Who was the first of Elvis's movie co-stars to share equal billing with him?

12. ANSWERS

1. Marion Keisker, at Memphis Recording Service

2. "My Happiness"

3. Sun Records

4. "That's All Right (Mama)"/"Blue Moon of Kentucky"

5. Dewey Phillips of WHBQ in Memphis

6. Sleepy Eye John, of WHHM in Memphis

7. "Mystery Train"/"I Forgot To Remember To Forget"

8. "Heartbreak Hotel"/"I Was The One"

9. Pink

10. Bob Neal

11. 1956

12. Jailhouse Rock

13. Loving You

14. "Heartbreak Hotel"

15. (b)

16. "Loving You"

17. "Old Shep"

18. Ann-Margret, in **Viva Las Vegas**

19. Twenty-one

20. Ann-Margret

13. MILESTONES

Place these Presley career highlights in the chronological order in which they occurred.

1. Cuts first gold record

2. Inducted into the army

3. Retains Colonel Tom Parker as his personal manager

4. "Too Much" becomes his eighth million-seller in one year

5. Signs with RCA Victor Records

6. First motion picture opens

7. Marries long-time sweetheart

8. Appears for first time on national TV

9. Purchases Graceland mansion in Memphis

10. Mother dies

13. ANSWERS

1. (3) November, 1955

2. (5) December, 1955

3. (1) January 10, 1956

4. (8) January 28, 1956

5. (6) November, 1956

6. (4) May, 1957

7. (9) July, 1957

8. (2) March, 1958

9. (10) August, 1958

10. (7) May, 1967

14. SONG SETTINGS

1. What Hawaiian city does Elvis's "Rock-A-Hula Baby" come from?

2. Where is "Heartbreak Hotel" located?

3. What was the home state of the drummer boy who went "crash, boom, bang" in "Jailhouse Rock"?

4. In "G.I. Blues," what would Elvis rather be looking at than a view of the Rhine?

5. What "bright light city" is going to set Elvis's soul on fire?

6. What type of instrument does "King Creole" play in New Orleans?

7. Where is Elvis headed when he's "Ridin' the Rainbow"?

8. What city is Elvis describing when he sings "I Think I'm Gonna Like It Here"?

9. In "Hard Knocks," where does the lonesome whistle blow?

10. In what city is a poor baby child born "In the Ghetto"?

14. ANSWERS

1. Honolulu

2. Lonely Street

3. Illinois

4. An old, muddy Texas creek

5. Las Vegas ("Viva Las Vegas")

6. A guitar

7. Heaven

8. Acapulco, from the movie **Fun In Acapulco**

9. New York City to Mexico

10. Chicago

15. LOVE ME TENDER

1. How tall does a love grow "Wild In The Country"?

2. In "Easy Come, Easy Go," what is in the air?

3. What is Elvis doing while he's "Ridin' the Rainbow"?

4. In "Love Me Tender," what will happen to Elvis's dreams?

5. What are Elvis and his baby going to "Patch It Up" with?

6. What two things does Elvis say to take in "Can't Help Falling In Love"?

7. In "Good Luck Charm," how much gold is Elvis's girl's love worth?

8. Why does Elvis have to "Follow That Dream"?

9. In "Surrender," what tells the story of Elvis's and his darling's love?

10. How does Elvis feel when he's apart from his girl in "I Want You, I Need You, I Love You"?

11. In what song does Elvis declare his love won't wait?

12. What time is it when Elvis and his girl pull down the blinds, kick out the maid, and hang a sign reading "Do Not Disturb" on the door?

13. What does Elvis have turned up high and turned down low in "I Need Your Love Tonight"?

14. In "Puppet On A String," how does Elvis say to handle his heart?

15. What is Elvis's goal in "Pledging My Love"?

15. ANSWERS

1. To the sky

2. Crazy love

3. Living to love

4. They will all be fulfilled

5. A lotta love

6. His hand and his whole life

7. All there is on earth

8. To find the love he needs

9. The stars

10. Like he's dying

11. "It's Now Or Never"

16. SUBTITLE SUBTERFUGE

What Elvis singles contain the following seldom-used subtitle phrases?

1. "The Vicious Circle"

2. "That's How I Will Be"

3. "What You Never Had"

4. "Kaunai"

5. "Let Me Be Your"

6. "From Paradise"

7. "To A Heart That's True"

8. "To Me"

9. "Something Old, Something New,
Something Borrowed"

10. "Drums Of Hawaii"

71

16. ANSWERS

1. "In The Ghetto"

2. "Any Way You Want Me"

3. "How Can You Lose"

4. "Island Of Love"

5. "Teddy Bear"

6. "So Close Yet So Far"

7. "Don't Be Cruel"

8. "Santa, Bring My Baby Back"

9. "Something Blue"

10. "Drums Of The Islands"

17. SCREEN ROMANCES

1. This leggy dancing sensation appeared as Elvis's girlfriend, Lil, in **G.I. Blues.**

2. Star of television's "The Ghost And Mrs. Muir," she created the role of Elvis's probation officer, Irene Sperry, in **Wild In The Country.**

3. She co-starred as Elvis's girlfriend in two films—**Blue Hawaii** and **Kid Galahad.**

4. This sex goddess of James Bondian fame played Elvis's gal-pal, Margarita Dauphine, in **Fun In Acapulco.**

5. A member of Donna Reed's TV family, this beauty co-starred with Elvis in three films—**Girl Happy, Spinout,** and **Clambake.**

6. Elly May Clampett in television's rural sitcom "The Beverly Hillbillies," she portrayed Frankie opposite Elvis's Johnny in **Frankie And Johnny.**

7. The singing-swinging daughter of a famous singing sensation, she was Susan Jacks, Elvis's love interest, in **Speedway.**

8. This vivacious singer-dancer starred as Elvis's competitive girlfriend, Rusty Martin, in **Viva Las Vegas.**

9. A former British debutante, this shapely, blond-haired lovely was Elvis's girl, Judy Hudson, in **Paradise—Hawaiian Style.**

10. She gave Elvis his first screen kiss as Cathy in **Love Me Tender.**

17. ANSWERS

1. Juliet Prowse

2. Hope Lange

3. Joan Blackman

4. Ursula Andress

5. Shelley Fabares

6. Donna Douglas

7. Nancy Sinatra

8. Ann-Margret

9. Suzanna Leigh

10. Debra Paget

18. ANIMAL INSTINCTS

1. What type of insect did Elvis get "stung" by?

2. Why isn't Elvis's "Hound Dog" his friend?

3. In "G.I. Blues," what would Elvis blow his next month's pay to buy?

4. How could birds learn to fly in "Rock-A-Hula Baby"?

5. In "Teddy Bear," what two animals does Elvis **not** want to be?

6. What do Elvis's friends say he's acting queer as in "All Shook Up"?

7. What animal will Elvis squeeze you tighter than because he's "Stuck On You"?

8. What type of fish jumping on a pole does "King Creole" look like?

9. In "Mean Woman Blues," what kind of animal died of fright when she crossed its path last night?

10. Although he's never kissed either a bear or a goon, what does Elvis claim he can shake in "Party"?

18. ANSWERS

1. A bee

2. Because he never has caught a rabbit

3. A piece of Texas cow

4. By watching how Elvis's baby can go

5. A tiger and a lion

6. A bug

7. A grizzly bear

8. A catfish

9. A black cat

10. A chicken

19. INFATUATIONS

1. What was the name of Elvis's high school sweetheart who later became the president of his first fan club?

2. Who was the Las Vegas chorus girl who spent Christmas with the Presley family in 1956?

3. What Las Vegas stripper was Elvis romantically linked with in 1957?

4. What was the name of the former Miss Texas who was seeing Elvis off-screen while co-starring with him in **Jailhouse Rock?**

5. What sixteen-year-old German fraulein was Elvis's steady date when he first reported for army duty overseas?

6. Which one of Presley's film co-stars

was seriously dating Frank Sinatra at the same time she was carrying on a romance with Elvis?

7. What was the name of the blond Miss Georgia Elvis briefly dated?

8. What former Miss Tennessee-U.S.A. was Elvis's steady girl?

9. What was her baby-like pet name for Elvis?

10. Which one of Elvis's girlfriends jilted him for actor James Caan?

19. ANSWERS

1. Dixie Locke

2. Dorothy Harmony

3. Tempest Storm

4. Anne Heyland

5. Margrit Buergin

6. Juliet Prowse

7. Diane Goodman

8. Linda Thompson

9. "Little Baby Bunting"

10. Sheila Ryan

20. TITLE TEASERS

Fill in the missing word in the titles of these Elvis single record releases.

1. "Mama Liked The _____"

2. "Big _____ Man"

3. "_____ Fit The Battle"

4. "Kiss Me _____"

5. "_____ Love Affair"

6. "I Love You _____"

7. "A Mess Of _____"

8. "Milky _____ Way"

9. "If I Can _____"

10. "U.S. _____"

11. "An _____ Trilogy"

12. "Kentucky _____"

13. "The Wonder of _____"

14. "_____ It Up"

15. "I Forgot To Remember To _____"

16. "_____ Letters"

17. "She's Not _____"

18. "The Sound Of Your _____"

19. "Trying To Get To _____"

20. "Mystery _____"

20. ANSWERS

1. Roses

2. Boss

3. Joshua

4. Quick

5. One-Sided

6. Because

7. Blues

8. White

9. Dream

10. Male

11. American

12. Rain

13. You

14. Patch

15. Forget

16. Love

17. You

18. Cry

19. You

20. Train

21. MAKING THE SCENE

In which Elvis films did the following scenes take place?

1. Elvis's wrists are tied together and he is unjustly flogged.

2. Elvis spanks a teenaged girl who's just wrecked a jeep.

3. Elvis dives off a 136-foot-high cliff into a roaring surf.

4. Elvis sings "Wooden Heart" to a group of puppets in a show.

5. Elvis punches out a man wearing a monster mask who breaks into his girl-friend's room.

6. An overmatched Elvis kayoes Sugar-

boy Romero to win the Labor Day prize fight.

7. Elvis tunnels under and into his girl's jail cell, only to discover that she has already been "bailed out" by her rich father.

8. Elvis's lucky cricket saves his life when he is accidentally shot by his jealous girlfriend while he is singing a song.

9. Elvis's former gang members show him a phony "Wanted" poster declaring him guilty of stealing a treasured Mexican cannon.

10. Elvis is chased into the ocean by a Great Dane.

11. While riding a train to college, Elvis cries tears of joy when he discovers that a story he wrote has been published in a magazine.

12. Elvis wins the Charlotte 600 motor race and collects enough prize money to pay off his debts.

13. Elvis discovers a treasure chest in the

hull of a sunken ship while deactivating an underwater mine.

14. Elvis is blackmailed into plotting the assassination of a king.

15. Elvis beats up the trappers who had insulted his Indian mother.

21. ANSWERS

1. Jailhouse Rock

2. Blue Hawaii

3. Fun In Acapulco

4. G.I. Blues

5. Tickle Me

6. Kid Galahad

7. Girl Happy

8. Frankie And Johnny

9. Charro!

10. Live A Little, Love A Little

11. Wild In The Country

12. Speedway

13. Easy Come, Easy Go

14. Harum Scarum

15. Flaming Star

22. IT'S A MATTER OF TIME

1. How long will Elvis love you in "I Want You, I Need You, I Love You"?

2. In "It's Now Or Never," when will it be too late?

3. When did "Johnnie" promise "Frankie" he'd be home from his night of gambling?

4. When is it time to "Follow That Dream"?

5. How long has Elvis been "Trying To Get To You"?

6. When does Elvis "Need Your Love" in this 1959 hit?

7. When does "King Creole" stop playing?

8. How long does Elvis smooch with his "Kissin' Cousins"?

9. When is the only time Elvis's gal is happy in "Mean Woman Blues"?

10. At what time of day does Elvis walk to the beach to express his "Never-Ending" love?

11. What will time unravel if Elvis and his girl don't "Patch It Up"?

12. Although it's a long, lonely night, what can Elvis and his baby "make" if they try?

13. When will Elvis be kissing his girl's lips in "Ain't That Loving You Baby"?

14. When did Elvis's letter come back to him marked "Return To Sender"?

15. When does Elvis say he will be back in "See See Rider"?

22. ANSWERS

1. Eternally

2. Tomorrow

3. Before dawn

4. When your heart becomes restless

5. Ever since he read your letter

6. Tonight ("I Need Your Love Tonight")

7. When his guitar breaks

8. All night

9. When she's mad

10. Sunset

11. Their dreams

12. The morning ("We Can Make The Morning")

13. Before the sun sets

14. Bright and early the next morning

15. Fall

23. ELVIS ETCETERA

1. What was the nickname given to Elvis's high school buddies who served as his bodyguards, chauffeurs, errand boys, and constant companions?

2. What was the name of Elvis's longtime back-up singing quartet both on records and movies?

3. What is the name of Elvis's octogenarian grandmother?

4. What type of figurines and symbols are on the front gates of Elvis's Memphis mansion, Graceland?

5. On what famous Memphis Street is Graceland situated?

6. What was the name of Elvis's personal physician?

7. Who was Elvis's private plane named after?

8. Approximately how many Elvis fan clubs were in operation when "the Pelvis" was at his peak?

9. What personal service did Homer "Gil" Gilliland perform on a regular basis for Elvis?

10. What code name did Ann-Margret use when she came to visit Elvis at Graceland?

11. What code name did Elvis himself use for his personal calls and mail?

12. What cost Elvis between $15,000 and $20,000 and has a sofa bed, a television, a refrigerator, a hi-fi, and a burglar alarm in it?

13. What was Elvis's favorite make of motorcycle?

14. Of those he worked with, who was Elvis's favorite actress?

15. What does the name "Elvis" mean?

23. ANSWERS

1. The "Memphis Mafia"

2. The Jordanaires

3. Minnie Mae Presley

4. Two green figurines of Elvis playing the guitar, along with musical notes

5. Elvis Presley Boulevard

6. Dr. George Nichopoulos

7. His daughter, Lisa Marie

8. Five thousand

9. He was Elvis's personal hairdresser

10. "Bunny"

11. "John Burrows"

12. His customized van

13. Harley Davidson

14. Shelley Fabares

15. "All-wise," from the Norse "Alviss"

24. TV TWISTIN'

1. On what summer-replacement series did Elvis make his first national television appearance?

2. Who were the hosts of this Jackie Gleason-produced program?

3. Which one of the show's hosts was credited with having "discovered" Elvis?

4. When did "the King" make his historic network debut?

5. On what network did the program air?

6. What million-selling hit did Elvis introduce in his first TV outing?

7. How many subsequent appearances did Elvis make on this variety series?

8. How much was Elvis paid for each appearance?

9. What television pioneer hosted Elvis for two 1956 guest appearances?

10. Three months before he appeared on Ed Sullivan's Sunday night variety hour, Elvis turned up as the guest on a rival network's program. What was the name of this show?

11. To whom did Elvis sing his hit song, "Hound Dog"?

12. What was so unusual about the outfit Elvis wore when he sang this song?

13. What western character did Elvis portray in a comedy skit featuring the show's host, Andy Griffith, and Imogene Coca?

14. How many times did Elvis appear on Ed Sullivan's "Toast Of The Town"?

15. How much was he paid for these appearances?

16. What distinguished British actor was subbing for host Ed Sullivan when Elvis made his first appearance on "Toast Of The Town"?

17. On his first "Toast Of The Town" guest stint, Elvis appeared live from the CBS studios in Hollywood rather than from where the Sullivan program originated in New York. Why?

18. What three songs did Elvis sing in his first "Toast Of The Town" appearance?

19. What did Ed Sullivan say about Elvis when he introduced the controversial singer?

20. How did Sullivan instruct his cameramen to film Elvis during the singing of his numbers?

21. After he sang this song on the Sullivan show, it became the only song never released as a single that made the national singles chart. Name that tune.

22. Who hosted the first television special

Elvis appeared in after returning from the army?

23. How much was Elvis paid for the 1968 Christmas TV special that resurrected his faltering career?

24. What was the name of Elvis's knock-out concert performance broadcast by NBC on April 4, 1973?

25. What distinguishing outfit did he wear for this inspired performance?

24. ANSWERS

1. "Stage Show"

2. Tommy and Jimmy Dorsey

3. Tommy Dorsey

4. January 28, 1956

5. CBS

6. "Heartbreak Hotel"

7. Five

8. $1,250

9. Milton Berle

10. "The Steve Allen Show"

11. A basset hound

12. He was wearing a tuxedo

13. "Tumbleweed"

14. Three times

15. $50,000

16. Charles Laughton

17. Elvis was busy filming the movie "Love Me Tender" in Hollywood

18. "Hound Dog," "Don't Be Cruel," and "Reddy Teddy"

19. "I don't know what he does, but it drives people crazy"

20. From the waist up

21. "Love Me"

22. Frank Sinatra

23. One million dollars

24. "Elvis: Aloha From Hawaii"

25. A white jumpsuit

25. FLIP SIDES

Match the "A" side of each single with its "B" or flip side.

1. "Jailhouse Rock"

2. "Stuck On You"

3. "Blue Suede Shoes"

4. "Teddy Bear"

5. "That's All Right (Mama)"

6. "I Got Stung"

7. "A Big Hunk O' Love"

8. "All Shook Up"

9. "Love Me Tender"

10. "Shake, Rattle, And Roll"

11. "I'm Counting On You"

12. "Too Much"

13. "It's Now Or Never"

14. "Hound Dog"

15. "Can't Help Falling In Love"

(a) "Playing For Keeps"

(b) "Any Way You Want Me"

(c) "Blue Moon Of Kentucky"

(d) "Lawdy, Miss Clawdy"

(e) "A Mess Of Blues"

(f) "Treat Me Nice"

(g) "One Night"

(h) "My Wish Came True"

(i) "Tutti Frutti"

(j) "I Got A Woman"

(k) "Don't Be Cruel"

(l) "Rock-A-Hula Baby"

(m) "Fame And Fortune"

(n) "That's When Your Heartaches Begin"

(o) "Loving You"

25. ANSWERS

1. (f)

2. (m)

3. (i)

4. (o)

5. (c)

6. (g)

7. (h)

8. (n)

9. (b)

10. (d)

11. (j)

12. (a)

13. (e)

14. (k)

15. (l)

8. Only three of Elvis's films lost money.

26. PLEASE BE TRUE

Indicate whether the following statements about Elvis are True or False.

1. Elvis couldn't read music.

2. Elvis recorded the first album to sell over a million copies.

3. During his early years, Elvis often performed in a bright orange jacket.

4. Elvis was far-sighted.

5. Elvis was a sworn officer of the law.

6. Elvis had a passion for buying Jaguars.

7. Elvis enjoyed his nickname "the Pelvis."

8. Only three of Elvis's films lost money at the box office.

9. It was estimated that Elvis had sold 100 million records at the time of his death.

10. Elvis was a deeply religious person.

26. ANSWERS

1. True

2. True

3. False. He wore a pink jacket

4. False. He was near-sighted

5. True. He was sworn in September 1, 1970, as a Shelby County non-salaried deputy sheriff. He was also given a federal narcotics officer's badge by President Nixon.

6. False. Elvis collected Cadillacs

7. False. He didn't care for it

8. False. All of Elvis's films were money-makers

9. False. He sold more than 600 million records

10. True

27. RECORD RIOT

1. What two natural disasters are mentioned in "Way Down"?

2. On what kind of morning is a poor little child born "In The Ghetto"?

3. According to Elvis, whose mother must have been good looking, too?

4. What is Elvis living on as he tries to find the "Pieces Of My Life"?

5. What are the six songs referred to in "Raised On Rock"?

6. What lie did they tell about Elvis's "Hound Dog"?

7. What color are the desk clerks wearing at "Heartbreak Hotel"?

8. In "G.I. Blues," what does Elvis eat for chow?

9. What is possible if you'll "Only Believe"?

10. Who played the saxophone while all the inmates danced to the "Jailhouse Rock"?

11. What sweet sound saved the wretch like me?

12. What does Elvis wear around his wrist in "A Big Hunk O' Love"?

13. In "I Was The One," what didn't Elvis teach her to do?

14. What type of dessert does "King Creole" sing about?

15. Who's knocking on the door at Elvis's "Party"?

27. ANSWERS

1. A tidal wave and fires

2. A cold and gray morning in Chicago

3. "T-R-O-U-B-L-E"

4. Songs his friends wrote for him to sing

5. "Honky Tonk," "Hound Dog," "Johnny B. Goode," "Chain Gang," "Love Is Strange," and "Knock On Wood"

6. That he was high-classed

7. Black

8. Black pumpernickel and hassenpfeffer

9. All things

10. Spider Murphy

11. "Amazing Grace"

12. A rabbit's foot

13. Lie

14. A jelly roll

15. Honky Tonky Joe

28. CASTING CALL

Match the actor with the role he created in an Elvis film.

1. Charles Bronson

2. Harry Morgan

3. Richard Egan

4. Burgess Meredith

5. Gary Lockwood

6. Rudy Vallee

7. Walter Matthau

8. Alejandro Rey

9. Bill Bixby

10. Will Hutchins

11. Michael Ansara

12. Regis Toomey

13. Jack Albertson

14. Mickey Shaughnessy

15. Arthur O'Connell

(a) Hank Houghton, Elvis's scheming cellmate in **Jailhouse Rock**

(b) Tom Wilson, the water-ski instructor Elvis trades places with in **Clambake**

(c) Charlie Lightcloud, Elvis's henpecked father in **Stay Away, Joe**

(d) Lew Nyack, Elvis's fight trainer in **Kid Galahad**

(e) Racketeer boss Maxie Fields in **King Creole**

(f) Lt. Vance Reno, Elvis's eldest brother in **Love Me Tender**

(g) Evil Prince Dragna in **Harum Scarum**

(h) Elvis's "Pop" in **Follow That Dream**

(i) Mr. Penlow, Elvis's straightlaced boss in **Live A Little, Love A Little**

(j) Kenny Donford, Elvis's best friend and business manager in **Speedway**

(k) Father Gibbons in **Change of Habit**

(l) Moreno, Elvis's lifeguard rival in **Fun In Acapulco**

(m) Danny Burke, Elvis's pilot sidekick in **It Happened At The World's Fair**

(n) Captain Robert Salbo, Elvis's commanding officer in **Kissin' Cousins**

(o) Cully, Elvis's piano-playing buddy in **Frankie And Johnny**

Elvis' home town watches him "shake, rattle, and roll" at the Mississippi-Alabama State Fair (1956)

**Elvis talks backstage with Ed Sullivan before his controversial te
vision appearance on "Toast of the Town" (1957)**

**Elvis talks over a scene with co-star Debra Paget on the set of th
movie** *Love Me Tender* **(1956)**

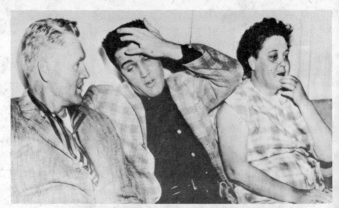

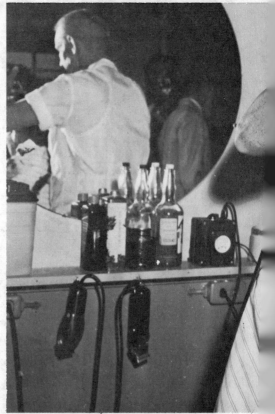

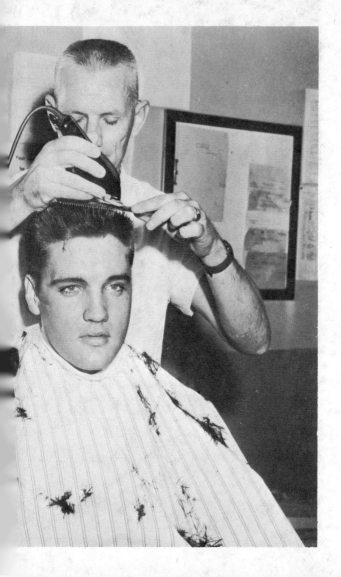

A happy Elvis is discharged from the Army (1960)

(opposite) Elvis finally gets "hitched" (1967)

Elvis as he looked three
months before the end
(1977)

28. ANSWERS

1. (d)

2. (o)

3. (f)

4. (c)

5. (m)

6. (i)

7. (e)

8. (l)

9. (j)

10. (b)

11. (g)

12. (k)

13. (n)

14. (a)

15. (h)

29. ARE YOU LONESOME TONIGHT?

1. Who is loneliness's first companion in "We Can Make The Morning"?

2. Where does "Lonely Man" roam?

3. What does Elvis pray for now that he knows life without his girl has been too lonely too long?

4. Where is Elvis sitting all alone in "Don't Be Cruel"?

5. How lonely does Elvis feel at "Heartbreak Hotel"?

6. Where will Elvis keep his girl's picture to pretend he's not alone after she leaves the "Heart Of Rome"?

7. What unfulfilled promise to himself has made Elvis blue and lonely in "I

Forgot To Remember To Forget"?

8. Why isn't "Poor Boy" lonesome and blue?

9. When is the only time "We Call On Him"?

10. Why does Elvis want to take away the aroma of flowers and hide the embraces of young lovers?

29. ANSWERS

1. Darkness

2. Town to town

3. "One Night" with you

4. At home

5. So lonely he could die

6. By his pillow

7. To forget that he and his girl ever met

8. Because he has a dolly like you

9. When we're lonely

10. Because "They Remind Me Too Much Of You"

30. IN CONCERT

1. What theme song heralded Elvis's grand entrance at each of his concerts?
2. In what Academy Award—winning movie was this music originally heard?

3. What was Elvis's finger-snappin', toe-tappin' opening concert number?

4. What did Elvis wipe his perspiration off with and toss to his screaming admirers during his emotionally-charged performances?

5. What love ballad concluded his concerts?

6. What comedian was given top billing over Elvis when the latter "bombed" playing Las Vegas's Frontier Hotel in 1956?

7. On March 26, 1961, Elvis performed what was to be his final live concert for over eight years. Where did he stage this farewell concert?

8. Who bought the first ticket to this benefit concert?

9. Where did Elvis make his dramatic comeback concert performance on July 31, 1969?

10. What was the name of the black female trio who provided the back up for Elvis during this career-resurrecting performance?

11. Elvis was the second performer to appear at this international cabaret. Who was the first?

12. Which Elvis film featured his sizzling Las Vegas concert appearance in August of 1970?

13. In what city did Elvis perform his final concert?

14. Following his 1969 return to the con-

cert scene, approximately how many public appearances did Elvis make a year?

15. About how much did Elvis gross for each of his concerts?

30. ANSWERS

1. "Also Sprach Zarathustra"

2. **2001: A Space Odyssey**

3. "See See Rider"

4. Nylon scarves

5. "Can't Help Falling In Love"

6. Sheckey Greene

7. Pearl Harbor, Hawaii

8. Elvis

9. The Las Vegas International Hotel (now the Las Vegas Hilton)

10. The Sweet Inspirations

11. Barbra Streisand

12. **That's The Way It Is**

13. Mobile, Alabama

14. Fifty

15. $100,000

31. JUKEBOX JUMBLE

How many of Elvis's hit singles can you find hidden in this maze of alphabet jibberish?

```
A B A N O R A P R E S E Y A D D A I L O
W E N O Z E M I E S A V U F O R I R K S
O W E S E M O N E Y H O N E Y A L A M E
O A T H E A L O V E L E T T E R S I T S
D R O O Y S O P U G A W I H A I P S U N
E S T U C K O N Y O U Y F A T E L E N A
N O O N A S U R R E N D E R O M E D I D
H A N D I U G H U P A R E Y O A T O K E
E S A D O S E A L O M A F O M I S N E Y
A I B O R P A T C H I T U P U N P R Y S
R M A G A I N O D U V A F E C O I O V E
T L I R Y C E K O N E N I G H T N C W S
A E L O S I V E N U S O R A I L O K A N
O A M Y B O Y A T M O O D Y B L U E Y E
O V E R A N S H O B Y A R O A S T A D Y
B I Q U I T H E G U I T A R M A N I O E
A N U S O M E M O R I E S H E L A C W A
Z Y F A N Y E S T O P L I A R O N O N D
A S O D E E K I H A L O V I N G Y O U R
P E M A B R E N Y D E W O N E W E G R Y
```

131

31. ANSWERS

```
A B A N O R A P R E S E Y A D D A I L O
W E N O Z E M I E S A V U F O R I R K S
O W E S E M O N E Y H O N E Y A L A M E
O A T H E A L O V E L E T T E R S I T S
D R O O Y S O P U G A W I H A I P S U N
E S T U C K O N Y O U Y F A T E L E N A
N O O N A S U R R E N D E R O M E D I D
H A N D I U G H U P A R E Y O A T O K E
E S A D O S E A L O M A F O M I S N E Y
A I B O R P A T C H I T U P U N P R Y S
R M A G A I N O D U V A F E C O I O V E
T L I R Y C E K O N E N I G H T N C W S
A E L O S I V E N U S O R A I L O K A N
O A M Y B O Y A T M O O D Y B L U E Y E
O V E R A N S H O B Y A R O A S T A D Y
B I Q U I T H E G U I T A R M A N I O E
A N U S O M E M O R I E S H E L A C W A
Z Y F A N Y E S T O P L I A R O N O N D
A S O D E E K I H A L O V I N G Y O U R
P E M A B R E N Y D E W O N E W E G R Y
```

32. PICTURE PROMOS

Name the Elvis movies that featured the following promotional teases.

1. "Watch Elvis Click With All These Chicks"

2. "Elvis Feudin' . . . Elvis Lovin' . . . Elvis Swingin' "

3. "The Red, White, And Blue Star-Bright Show Of The Year!"

4. "A Film About **Him**"

5. "Elvis Elvis Takes Mod Mod Europe By Song As He Swings Into A Brand New Adventure Filled With Dames, Diamonds, Discotheques, And Danger!"

6. "Half-Breed Torn Between Two Loyal-

ties, Two Loves—And Fighting To Save Them Both!"

7. "Ecstatic Romance . . . Exotic Dances . . . Exciting Music In The World's Lushest Paradise Of Song"

8. "Mr. Rock 'N' Roll In The Story He Was Born To Play!"

9. "On His Neck He Wore The Brand Of A Killer. On His Hip He Wore Vengeance."

10. "1001 Swingin' Nights As Elvis Brings The Big Beat To Bagdad In A Riotous, Rockin' Rollin' Adventure Spoof!!!"

11. "It's The 'Go-Go' Guy And That 'Bye-Bye' Gal!"

12. "Elvis Presley Packs The Screen's Biggest Wallop . . . With The Gals . . . With The Gloves . . . With The Guitar"

13. "The Swingin'-est Elvis! + Girls + Songs . . . Who Could Ask For Anything More?"

14. "Could He Change Her Life, Could She

Forget Her Vows And Follow Her Heart ..."

15. "Elvis Is Kissin' Cousins Again—And Also Friends, Friends Of Friends, And Even Some Perfect Strangers!"

16. "Elvis Jumps With The Campus Crowd To Make The Beach 'Ball' Bounce!!!"

17. "Elvis! Excitement! Adventure Under The Sea! Singin' . . . Scuba-Divin' . . . Swingin ..."

18. "It's Elvis Barreling . . . Biking . . . Bikini-ing And Belting Out That Wild Presley Beat"

19. "It's Elvis With His Foot On The Gas And No Brakes On The Fun"

20. "All Elvis Breaks Loose In The Swingin', Swayin', Luau-ing South Seas"

32. ANSWERS

1. Live A Little, Love A Little

2. Kissin' Cousins

3. G.I. Blues

4. That's The Way It Is

5. Double Trouble

6. Flaming Star

7. Blue Hawaii

8. Love Me Tender

9. Charro!

10. Harum Scarum

11. Viva Las Vegas

33. COLOR ME BLUE

1. What color Yuletide will Elvis's girl enjoy while he's pining away over a "Blue Christmas" without her?

2. Which one of the following songs was **not** featured in the movie **Blue Hawaii?** (a) "Moonlight Swim" (b) "Slicin' Sand" (c) "Ito Eats" (d) "Drums Of The Islands"

3. Of his girl or his "Blue Guitar," the one Elvis chooses.

4. What six things will Elvis let you do to him if you lay off of his "Blue Suede Shoes"?

5. What type of "G.I. Blues" is Elvis suffering from?

138

6. Why do lonely lovers go to "Blue River"?

7. Why isn't "Poor Boy" blue?

8. What kind of "Boogie" did Elvis sing about in his third professional recording?

9. Of "Indescribably," "Uncontrollably," or "Unbelievably," the "Blue" Elvis felt in a 1967 single release.

10. In what song from the film **Kissin' Cousins** does Elvis kick both his shoes and his blues off?

33. ANSWERS

1. A white Christmas

2. (d)

3. His "Blue Guitar"

4. Knock him down, step on his face, slander his name, burn his house, steal his car, and drink his cider from his old fruit jar

5. Occupation "G.I. Blues"

6. To cry away their tears

7. Because he has a dolly like you

8. "Milkcow Blues Boogie"

9. "Indescribably Blue"

10. "Barefoot Ballad"

34. YOU'RE IN THE ARMY NOW!

1. What movie was Elvis in the process of filming when he was drafted?

2. How did producer Hal Wallis manage to complete the picture?

3. In what year was Elvis inducted into the army?

4. How old was he at the time?

5. In what city did Elvis's swearing-in take place?

6. After his induction, Elvis was sent to Fort Chaffee, Arkansas. What historic event occurred there on March 25, 1958?

7. What was Elvis's widely-publicized army serial number?

8. Where did Elvis receive his mandatory eight weeks of basic training?

9. On September 19, 1958, Elvis sailed off to his overseas army assignment. What Presley hit did the band play as a send-off?

10. What was the name of the singer-actress who was Elvis's girlfriend at the time he was shipped overseas?

34. ANSWERS

1. **King Creole**

2. Elvis requested and was granted a deferment to finish work on the movie

3. 1958 (March 24)

4. Twenty-three

5. Memphis

6. Elvis's greased-back ducktail was whittled down to a regulation G.I. crewcut

7. ASN 53310761

8. Fort Hood, Texas

9. "All Shook Up"

10. Anita Wood

35. SOUNDTRACK SELECTIONS

Which Presley movies featured the following sets of songs?

1. "I Got Lucky"; "King Of The Whole Wide World"; "This Is Living"

2. "Return To Sender"; "A Boy Like Me, A Girl Like You"; "I Didn't Want To"

3. "Trouble"; "Crawfish"; "As Long As I Have You"

4. "All That I Am"; "Adam And Evil"; "Tomorrow Is A Long Time"

5. "I Slipped, I Stumbled, I Fell"; "Lonely Man"; "In My Way"

6. "El Toro"; "Bossa Nova Baby"; "The Bullfighter Was A Lady"

144

7. "Blue River"; "Could I Fall In Love"; "Never-Ending"

8. "Treat Me Nice"; "Baby, I Don't Care"; "Young And Beautiful"

9. "Guitar Man"; "Big Boss Man"; "How Can You Lose What You Never Had?"

10. "Teddy Bear"; "Lover Doll"; "Got A Whole Lot O' Livin' To Do"

11. "Let Me"; "Poor Boy"; "We're Gonna Move"

12. "Angel"; "What A Wonderful Life"; "I'm Not The Marrying Kind"

13. "Hard Knocks"; "Wheels On My Heels"; "Big Love Big Heartache"

14. "Pocketful of Rainbows"; "Didja Ever?"; "Shoppin' Around"

15. "Shout It Out"; "Come Along"; "Please Don't Stop Loving Me"

16. "They Remind Me Too Much Of You"; "One Broken Heart For Sale"; "I'm Falling In Love Tonight"

17. "Put The Blame On Me"; "I Feel That I've Known You Forever"; "Dirty, Dirty Feeling"

18. "Puppet On A String"; "Do Not Disturb"; "Spring Fever"

19. "One Boy, Two Little Girls"; "Long Lonely Highway"; "Once Is Enough"

20. "So Close, Yet So Far"; "Mirage"; "Animal Instinct"

35. ANSWERS

1. Kid Galahad

2. Girls! Girls! Girls!

3. King Creole

4. Spinout

5. Wild In The Country

6. Fun In Acapulco

7. Double Trouble

8. Jailhouse Rock

9. Clambake

10. Loving You

11. Love Me Tender

36. LIGHTS! CAMERA! ACTION!

1. During the aftermath of what war did **Love Me Tender** take place?

2. What was Elvis's meat-and-potatoes punch in **Kid Galahad?**

3. What crime sent Elvis to prison in **Jailhouse Rock?**

4. What phobia did Elvis suffer from in **Fun In Acapulco?**

5. What did it mean when you saw your "Flaming Star"?

6. What was the "King Creole"?

7. Where did Elvis, his "pop," and adopted siblings choose to homestead in **Follow That Dream?**

8. What missing part did Elvis need to buy for his race car in **Viva Las Vegas?**

9. What did Frankie want Johnny to stop doing before she would marry him in **Frankie And Johnny?**

10. Where did Elvis work as a singing "Roustabout"?

11. What did the sunken treasure of Spanish pieces-of-eight turn out to be in **Easy Come, Easy Go?**

12. What big race did Elvis win in **Speedway?**

13. What was the name of the Mexican cannon Elvis rescued from an outlaw gang in **Charro!?**

14. Where did Elvis practice medicine in **Change Of Habit?**

15. What type of business did Elvis start with his buddy in **Paradise—Hawaiian Style?**

36. ANSWERS

1. The Civil War

2. A right

3. Manslaughter

4. A fear of heights

5. You were going to die

6. A New Orleans nightclub

7. On a Florida beach

8. An engine

9. Gambling

10. At a carnival

11. Copper coins

12. The Charlotte 600

13. Victory Gun

14. In the ghetto

15. A helicopter charter service

37. PUCKER UP!

1. In "Young Dreams," how often do Elvis's young lips want to kiss you?

2. What is Elvis "So Close, Yet So Far" from when he kisses his love?

3. In "Surrender," what is Elvis's heart burning with when he kisses his darling?

4. What will every kiss bring "As Long As I Have You"?

5. In what song does Elvis complain that his kissing cousin is a ripe pineapple?

6. How long does Elvis smooch with his "Kissin' Cousins"?

7. In "I Slipped, I Stumbled, I Fell,"

where does Elvis head after one crazy kiss?

8. In what song does Elvis ask his darling to kiss him and be his tonight?

9. What are Elvis's girl's kisses like in "All Shook Up"?

10. In "Stuck On You," what happens once Elvis catches you and the kissing starts?

11. How does Elvis answer himself when he wonders how many times his girl's lips have been kissed?

12. How does Elvis feel when your lips touch his in "Fame And Fortune"?

13. In "Big Hunk O' Love," what would Elvis have if you gave him one sweet kiss?

14. Who taught Elvis's girl how to kiss the way she kisses another man now?

15. What doesn't Elvis want his girl to say when he wants to kiss her?

37. ANSWERS

1. Morning, noon, and night

2. Paradise

3. A strange desire

4. A thrill

5. "Beach Boy Blues"

6. All night

7. For the skies

8. "It's Now Or Never"

9. A hot volcano

10. A team of wild horses wouldn't be able to tear you apart

11. "I Really Don't Want To Know"

12. Like a king

13. Everything his lucky charms could give him

14. "I Was The One"

15. "Don't"

38. THE FORMER MRS. PRESLEY

1. What is the name of Elvis's ex-wife?

2. What was her maiden name?

3. What is the color of her hair?

4. What color are her eyes?

5. What is her religion?

6. Where did she and Elvis first meet?

7. How old was she when she first started dating Elvis?

8. What was her father's occupation at the time?

9. In what year did she move in with Elvis and his parents at Graceland?

10. How many years did she live at Graceland before marrying Elvis?

11. How old was she when she became Elvis's bride?

12. How old was Elvis?

13. Where was the loving couple married?

14. What Presley hit song was played at their wedding?

15. How much did Elvis spend for their wedding breakfast?

16. Who was the only actor invited to the wedding?

17. Where did the couple spend their four-day honeymoon?

18. What was the name of the 163-acre Memphis ranch Elvis bought for himself and his bride?

19. How long did Elvis stay married?

20. Whom did Elvis's ex start dating after she split with her world-famous hubby?

38. ANSWERS

1. Priscilla

2. Beaulieu

3. Auburn

4. Gray

5. Catholic

6. In Bad Nauheim, Germany, when Elvis was stationed overseas in the army

7. Fourteen years old

8. A United States Air Force captain

9. 1960

10. Almost seven years

11. Twenty-one

12. Thirty-two

13. The Aladdin Hotel in Las Vegas

14. "Love Me Tender"

15. $100,000

16. Redd Foxx

17. Palm Springs

18. The "Circle G," named after Graceland

19. Six years

20. Her karate instructor, Mike Stone

39. ONE BROKEN HEART FOR SALE

1. Which one of the "Pieces Of My Life" does Elvis miss the most?

2. What happens to Elvis when "It's Midnight"?

3. Who is the life, pride, and joy of Elvis's life and the only reason he stays married to his wife?

4. What may happen someday after Elvis and his wife go their "Separate Ways"?

5. Where do gloomy, broken-hearted lovers go to cry?

6. What will happen "When I'm Over You"?

7. Who wants to pour out his heart to his

girl but instead just leaves word he said hello?

8. Of "You're A Heartbreaker," "That's When Your Heartaches Begin," and "One Broken Heart For Sale," the one Elvis first records for Sun Records

9. Why can't Elvis's girl break his heart anymore in "You're A Heartbreaker"?

10. Along what path does the "Blue River" flow?

39. ANSWERS

1. You

2. He misses you

3. "My Boy"

4. They may find another love

5. "Heartbreak Hotel"

6. My soul will be filled with darkness and light will never shine again

7. Jim ("Just Tell Her Jim Said Hello")

8. "You're A Heartbreaker"

9. Because he's found someone else to take her place

10. Along a path full of pain and heartache

40. CO-STAR CUTIES

Match the shapely leading lady with the movie in which she co-starred opposite Elvis.

1. Stella Stevens

2. Yvonne Craig

3. Annette Day

4. Michele Carey

5. Marlyn Mason

6. Tuesday Weld

7. Mary Tyler Moore

8. Carolyn Jones

9. Judy Tyler

10. Dodie Marshall

11. Mary Ann Mobley

12. Lizabeth Scott

13. Jocelyn Lane

14. Ina Balin

15. Anne Helm

(a) Speedway

(b) Change Of Habit

(c) Easy Come, Easy Go

(d) Loving You

(e) Charro!

(f) Clambake

(g) Follow That Dream

(h) Double Trouble

40. ANSWERS

1. (f)

2. (l)

3. (h)

4. (o)

5. (a)

6. (j)

7. (b)

8. (i)

9. (n)

10. (c)

11. (m)

12. (d)

13. (k)

14. (e)

15. (g)

41. GIRLS! GIRLS! GIRLS!

1. In "All Shook Up," what happens to Elvis's heart when he's near the girl he loves best?

2. What must Elvis believe when "A Boy Like Me" meets "A Girl Like You"?

3. Where did "Frankie" find "Johnnie" cheating with Nellie Bly?

4. Although she walks and talks like an angel, who does Elvis think his girl really is?

5. What will happen after she gets Elvis's heart going fast in "Spinout"?

6. Where did Uncle John hide when Aunt Mary caught him with "Long Tall Sally"?

7. What does Elvis think "T-R-O-U-B-L-E" looks like when she walks through the door of the dance hall?

8. What does Elvis say to color his complicated lady?

9. Why can't Elvis and his army buddies make a pass at the pretty frauleins in "G.I. Blues"?

10. Who really shakes the grass around when she begins to sway?

11. What was the name of the bull who was smitten with love when he found out that "The Bullfighter Was A Lady"?

12. Whom does Elvis say to grab by the hand to "Do The Clam"?

13. Where is Elvis's resistance when he's "Way Down" with his babe?

14. Whom does Elvis tell not to do what her big sister did?

15. Lawdy! What is the name of the "Miss" who looks so good to Elvis?

41. ANSWERS

1. His heart beats so fast it scares him to death

2. Wishes come true

3. In the barroom

4. The devil ("You're The Devil In Disguise")

5. She'll let him run out of gas

6. In the alley

7. Good-looking

8. "Moody Blue"

9. Because they're wearing signs warning the soldiers to keep off

42. PLAYING THE ROLE

In what movie did Elvis play the following characters?

1. Greg Nolan, a playboy pin-up photographer

2. John Carpenter, a ghetto doctor who works with nuns

3. Walter Hale, the manager of a traveling theatrical show

4. Steve Grayson, a champion race car driver heavily in debt to the Internal Revenue Service

5. Ted Jackson, a U.S. Navy frogman and demolition expert

6. Ross Carpenter, a nightclub singer

who wants to purchase his own fishing boat

7. Lonnie Beale, a singing rodeo star who works for a high-class dude ranch for girls

8. Walter Gulick, an ex-soldier who becomes a boxer

9. Scott Heyward, a millionaire's son who trades places with a poor water-ski instructor

10. Jess Wade, a former outlaw who goes straight

11. Charlie Rogers, a roving carnival handyman

12. Rusty Wells, the leader of a Chicago nightclub combo

13. Glenn Tyler, a rebellious probationer with a strong desire to become a writer

14. Johnny Tyronne, a Hollywood motion picture and recording star

15. Mike Windgren, an ex-trapeze artist who becomes a singer in a resort hotel

42. ANSWERS

1. Live A Little, Love A Little

2. Change Of Habit

3. The Trouble With Girls

4. Speedway

5. Easy Come, Easy Go

6. Girls! Girls! Girls!

7. Tickle Me

8. Kid Galahad

9. Clambake

10. Charro!

11. Roustabout

43. MORE KHAKI CAPERS

1. In what European country was Elvis stationed?

2. To what overseas division was Elvis assigned?

3. What was Elvis's job in the army?

4. Whom did Elvis live off-base with while he was stationed overseas?

5. Who was Elvis's steady date during the latter part of his army hitch?

6. What was the tender age of his army sweetheart?

7. At what Paris nightspot did Elvis make an impromptu stage appearance while stationed overseas in the army?

8. Elvis entered the service as a private. What rank did he hold when he was discharged?

9. How many years did Elvis serve in the army?

10. When was Elvis discharged from the service?

11. What famous entertainer threw a television party for Elvis to celebrate the rock 'n' roll star's return to civilian life?

12. What was the appropriate title of Elvis's first post-army record album?

13. A million orders had already been received for each of Elvis's first two post-army singles before they were even recorded. What were the titles of these golden hits?

14. What was Elvis's first number-one hit single after returning from the service?

15. What was the first movie Elvis starred in after his army days were over?

43. ANSWERS

1. Germany

2. The Third Armored Division

3. He drove a jeep

4. His father and grandmother (Minnie)

5. Priscilla Beaulieu (his future wife)

6. Fourteen

7. The Lido

8. Sergeant

9. Two

10. March 5, 1960

11. Frank Sinatra

12. "Elvis Is Back"

13. "Stuck On You" and "Fame And Fortune"

14. "Stuck On You"

15. G.I. Blues

44. I'M COUNTING ON YOU

1. How many of his babe's magic fingers have Elvis "Way Down"?

2. In "Jailhouse Rock," who told prisoner Number Three that he was the cutest jailbird he ever did see?

3. What caliber gun did "Frankie" go after "Johnnie" with because he was doing her wrong?

4. When Elvis marries his girl, how many people will live in their happy home in "I'm Left, You're Right, She's Gone"?

5. How many miles does Elvis figure he's walked tired, hungry, cold and wet taking his "Hard Knocks"?

6. What number will Elvis be betting on if his girlfriend will only "Come Along"?

7. In "T-R-O-U-B-L-E," what are Elvis's piano-playing hours at the dance hall?

8. What time will Elvis be buzzing around his sweet honeybee's hive in "I Got Stung!"?

9. How many times does Elvis demand that his girlfriend kiss him in "Treat Me Nice"?

10. In "Viva Las Vegas," how many pretty women are waiting out there living devil may care?

44. ANSWERS

1. A hundred

2. Number Forty-Seven

3. A .44

4. Two or three

5. A million miles

6. Number nine

7. From nine o'clock until half past one

8. At five

9. Twice

10. A thousand

45. ON LOCATION

Match the movie with its geographical setting.

1. King Creole

2. G.I. Blues

3. Harum Scarum

4. Frankie And Johnny

5. It Happened At The World's Fair

6. Spinout

7. Double Trouble

8. Charro!

9. Clambake

10. **Kissin' Cousins**

11. **Live A Little, Love A Little**

12. **Speedway**

13. **Girl Happy**

14. **Tickle Me**

15. **Love Me Tender**

(a) Miami Beach

(b) Seattle

(c) Belgium and Holland

(d) Mexico

(e) New Orleans

(f) Charlotte

(g) Santa Fe

(h) Zuni Wells

(i) Germany

(j) Tennessee

(k) Ft. Lauderdale

(l) Bagdad

(m) East Texas

(n) Mississippi

(o) Los Angeles

45. ANSWERS

1. (e)

2. (i)

3. (l)

4. (n)

5. (b)

6. (g)

7. (c)

8. (d)

9. (a)

10. (j)

11. (o)

12. (f)

13. (k)

14. (h)

15. (m)

46. SING IT AGAIN, ELVIS!

1. What was Elvis blamed for early in life in "You Gave Me A Mountain"?

2. What will Elvis stick to his girl like in "Stuck OnYou"?

3. How long does Elvis tell his bride he will love her in "Hawaiian Wedding Song"?

4. What does Elvis face in "My Way"?

5. What does Elvis ask his girl if she's sorry about in "Are You Lonesome Tonight"?

6. Why won't Elvis be hanging around his girl's door in "That's All Right (Mama)"?

7. What would Elvis beg and steal to feel in "Love Me"?

8. How far away from home is Elvis in "Early Morning Rain"?

9. Why won't Elvis let the evening get him down in "And I Love You So"?

10. What did Elvis used to pinch on "Little Sister" when she was younger?

46. ANSWERS

1. The fact that his mother had died at birth, leaving his father a widower

2. Glue

3. Forever

4. The final curtain

5. He asks her if she's sorry they drifted apart

6. Because he's leaving town

7. His girl's heart beating against his

8. A long way

9. Because his girl will be around

10. Her turned-up nose

47. LOVESICK LYRICS

1. In what song does Elvis sing that he would cry and feel sad, blue, and lonely if his girl ever left him?

2. What does every kiss bring "As Long As I Have You"?

3. In "A Big Hunk O' Love," how much is Elvis asking of his baby?

4. What does Elvis ask his girl if her heart is filled with in "Are You Lonesome Tonight"?

5. What makes Elvis break into a cold sweat in "I Got Stung!"?

6. Why doesn't Elvis care where his gal's gone in "I'm Left, You're Right, She's Gone"?

7. What two things does Elvis confess "I Really Don't Want To Know" about his girl's past?

8. How does Elvis's girl make love in "Mean Woman Blues"?

9. What did Elvis's date want to do at the drive-in movie in "Didja Ever"?

10. In "Don't Ask Me Why," what kind of love does Elvis have for his girl?

47. ANSWERS

1. "Love Me"

2. A thrill

3. Not much of her

4. Pain

5. A little peck behind his neck

6. Because he's fallen for you

7. How many other men have held her in their arms and how many other lips have kissed her

8. Without a smile

9. Watch the show

10. Not the kind he dreamed about, but the kind he can't live without

48. SCRAMBLED SINGLES

Unscramble the titles of these Elvis hit records.

1. DETYD REBA

2. TITUT TRUTIF

3. OGOD KORINC THONGIT

4. TELLIT TIRESS

5. SOSAB AVON ABYB

6. BATHERAKER THOLE

7. SIKINS SONUSIC

8. RHAD DAHEED MANOW

9. CUSSIPOUSI DIMSN

10. APETASER YAWS

11. HAULEJOIS CORK

12. TOND RYC DYADD

13. WYLAD SIMS LYCWAD

14. WHO ETRAG HOTU RAT

15. GRUNBIN VELO

48. ANSWERS

1. "Teddy Bear"

2. "Tutti Frutti"

3. "Good Rockin' Tonight"

4. "Little Sister"

5. "Bossa Nova Baby"

6. "Heartbreak Hotel"

7. "Kissin' Cousins"

8. "Hard Headed Woman"

9. "Suspicious Minds"

10. "Separate Ways"

11. "Jailhouse Rock"

12. "Don't Cry, Daddy"

13. "Lawdy, Miss Clawdy"

14. "How Great Thou Art"

15. "Burning Love"

49. PRESLEY POTPOURRI

1. How much did Elvis pay for his Graceland estate? (a) $1,000,000 (b) $100,000 (c) $500,000 (d) $5,000,000

2. Who, besides Elvis's mother and father, referred to the rock 'n' roll king as "my boy"?

3. What famous musical quartet once invited Elvis to join them as their fifth member?

4. What was Elvis's favorite song?

5. What was the name of the Broadway musical that was loosely based on Elvis's meteoric rise to rock 'n' roll stardom?

6. Who became one of Elvis's best friends

after he tried out for but failed to get a role in the film **Love Me Tender?**

7. Both sides of an Elvis single rose to number one on the 1956 record charts, marking the only time this has happened in recording history. What were the two sides of this double-gold Presley platter?

8. Which one of the following persons who had been close to Elvis during his lifetime did not attend the singer's funeral? (a) his father (b) his personal manager, Colonel Parker (c) his ex-wife (d) former co-star Ann-Margret

9. With what Hollywood starlet did Elvis carry on a "motorcycle romance" in 1956?

10. What did Elvis have installed next to the pool at his Graceland estate?

49. ANSWERS

1. (b)

2. Colonel Parker, his personal manager

3. The Beatles

4. "There's No Tomorrow"

5. **Bye Bye Birdie**

6. Nick Adams, who played Johnny Yuma in TV's "The Rebel"

7. "Hound Dog" and "Don't Be Cruel"

8. (b)

9. Natalie Wood

10. A jukebox

50. THE FINAL CURTAIN

1. What eye affliction plagued Elvis during his final years?

2. What was his final single record release?

3. What was the title of his last record album?

4. What was the date of Elvis's untimely death?

5. How old was he when he died?

6. What was listed as the official cause of his death?

7. At what hospital was Elvis pronounced dead?

8. What color funeral did Elvis want and get?

9. In typical Elvis fashion, what led his funeral procession through the streets of Memphis?

10. Where was Elvis first interred?

11. Where was Elvis finally laid to rest after security problems made it necessary to move his body?

12. Who was named as the executor of Elvis's estate?

13. Who were the principal beneficiaries named in Elvis's will?

14. How much of Elvis's estate was left to his ex-wife and his fiancee?

15. Who delivered the eulogy at Elvis's funeral?

50. ANSWERS

1. Glaucoma

2. "Way Down"

3. "Moody Blue"

4. August 17, 1977

5. Forty-two

6. Cardiac arrhythmia

7. Baptist Memorial Hospital

8. White

9. A fleet of white Cadillacs

10. Forest Hills Cemetery

11. Graceland

12. His father, Vernon

13. His father, daughter, and grandmother

14. Nothing was left to either one

15. Reverend Rex Humbard, television
    evangelist